G. Anderson Miller

Noble Martyrs of Kent

G. Anderson Miller

Noble Martyrs of Kent

ISBN/EAN: 9783337778712

Printed in Europe, USA, Canada, Australia, Japan

Cover: Foto ©Lupo / pixelio.de

More available books at **www.hansebooks.com**

NOBLE MARTYRS OF KENT

BY THE REV.
G. ANDERSON MILLER
ROCHESTER

FOREWORD BY THE REV.
H. TYDEMAN CHILVERS
SPURGEON'S TABERNACLE

MORGAN & SCOTT L^{TD.}
(OFFICE OF "The Christian")
12, PATERNOSTER BUILDINGS
LONDON   E.C. 4

PRINTED IN SCOTLAND

DEDICATED
TO THE REV.
W. FULLER GOOCH
MY FAITHFUL AND LOVING PASTOR
BEFORE BEING ORDAINED
TO THE MINISTRY OF CHRIST
AND
MY INSPIRING EXAMPLE
AND HELPFUL FRIEND
EVER SINCE

PREFACE

IN the course of a long ministry in the Cathedral city of Rochester, it has been my pleasurable duty to study Protestantism, also to speak and write on the same. Many friends have earnestly and repeatedly urged me to publish a handy book on the Protestant Martyrs of Kent, and after prayerful thought I have yielded to their requests. My sincere hope now is that they will not be disappointed.

With much gratitude I beg to acknowledge my indebtedness to the following writers and their works : *The Acts and Monuments of the Church* (*The Book of Martyrs*), by JOHN FOXE ; *History of Protestantism*, by Dr. J. A. WYLIE ; *Beauties of England and Wales*, by E. W. BRAYLEY ; *The Histories of Kent*, by ABEL, HASTED, IRELAND, FISHER, and WILDASH ; *The Perambulation of Kent*, by LAMBARD ; *Sketches of Rochester*, by PHIPPEN and EDWIN HARRIS ; *History of the Baptists*, by Dr. J. M. CRAMP ; *Story of the Baptists*, by Dr. J. C. CARLILE ; *History of the Weald of Kent,* by ROBERT FURLEY ; *Church History*, by THOMAS

FULLER; *Loyal and True*, by H. R. KNIGHT; *History of England*, by J. A. FROUDE; *A Short History of the English People*, by J. R. GREEN; *History of Dartford*, by JOHN DUNKIN; *History of Strood*, by H. SMETHAM; *A Saunter through Kent with Pen and Pencil*, by CHARLES IGGLESDEN.

The need for all to know the Truth and History of Protestantism is growingly evident, in view of the inroads of Roman Catholicism, then Anglo-Catholicism, and now Free Catholicism! The call to all true Protestants is to bear their own witness, and so prove themselves worthy successors of those who counted not their lives dear to them in their heroic testimony for Christ.

G. ANDERSON MILLER.

17 ROCHESTER AVENUE,
    ROCHESTER.

FOREWORD

"LEST we forget" is a quotation in the closing paragraph of this solemnly interesting book, and the words provide a most fitting reason for the publication of such a story. There is a great danger in these days of forgetting the cost at which our religious freedom and Reformation principles have come to us. Many are looking askance at the past, as though it contributed nothing to the present, and the satirical references made to our fathers, and their faith and fidelity, are sad signs of the times, and an ominous augury for the future. We owe a great debt to those worthies who counted not their lives dear or too precious to give for the sake of Christ and His Gospel.

Mr. G. Anderson Miller has done well in adding this contribution to Protestant literature; and surely none is more worthy of the honour to write it. The author has lived and served as a Baptist minister in Rochester for thirty-four years; he has built up a strong church of men and women who are true to the Gospel; and he has been the means of erecting a splendid block of buildings that stand as a monument to the power of his testimony. He was one of the many men sent by the late C. H. Spurgeon to do pioneer Baptist work in Kent. Everybody who knows G. Anderson Miller knows him as a stalwart for the truth of God.

The "Garden of England," as Kent is sometimes called, will appear in a new aspect to some of our young folk when they have read this book; for many do not realize how rich the county has been in faithful witness. The book should be placed in the hands of all members of our Young People's Societies and Bible Classes, to whom it is calculated to render valuable service.

This book is a most timely production; never did the people need, as now, to be instructed in the principles for which the martyrs died. They need to understand the character of those men and women of whom the world was not worthy and who were indeed "faithful unto death." Rome, too, should be seen in her true colours, for she has not changed. *Semper eadem* is her abiding motto.

There must be no parleying with Rome; she is the enemy of Protestantism. Rome is making a great effort to regain ascendancy in this country, and by Jesuitical means and methods she is not without success. Transubstantiation and the Mass are unscriptural and wicked; they rob the Saviour of His glory, and when taught pervert the meaning of Calvary's sacrifice. These practices are not only manifest in Roman Catholic circles, but many Anglo-Catholics are introducing them into the Church of England.

The Christians of Kent should do all in their power to circulate this book. It is adapted to awaken and stir the people from an increasing apathy and indifference to the advances of Romanism and the lethargy of Protestantism. May God speed the effort, and follow the circulation of the book with His Spirit's power and blessing, making it a means of revival in those things that give spiritual muscle and fibre, and put iron into the blood of Christian men and women. May it also be a means of stemming the tide of error and influence emanating from the mystic Babylon, especially in the honoured County of Kent.

H. TYDEMAN CHILVERS.

METROPOLITAN TABERNACLE,
   LONDON, S.E.

CONTENTS

	PAGE
I. INTRODUCTORY.	1
II. ROCHESTER— николаs Ridley	3
III. ROCHESTER (*Continued*)— Nicholas Hall—John Harpole—Joan Beach	13
IV. STROOD— William Wood—John Pemmell—John Bailey	15
V. DARTFORD— Christopher Waid—Nicholas Hall—Margery Polley	20
VI. SEVENOAKS— John Frith	25
VII. WROTHAM— John Corneford	32
VIII. MAIDSTONE— Edward Walker — Thomas Hitton — John Denley — John Newman, and Others	38
IX. TONBRIDGE— Joan Beach—Margery Polley	42

CONTENTS

	PAGE
X. STAPLEHURST— ALICE POTKINS—JOAN BRADBRIDGE—ALICE BENDEN	45
XI. SMARDEN— AGNES SNOTH — ANNE ALBRIGHT—JOAN SOLE—JOAN CATMER—JOHN LOMAS	48
XII. BIDDENDEN— WILLIAM WATERER—THOMAS STEPHENS	49
XIII. CRANBROOK— JOHN ARCHER—WILLIAM LOWICK	50
XIV. TENTERDEN— JOHN WADDON—WILLIAM CARDER—AGNES GREBIL—JOHN LOMAS, AND OTHERS	52
XV. ASHFORD AND HYTHE— JOHN BROWN — MATTHEW BRADBRIDGE—NICHOLAS FINAL	54
XVI. WYE AND FAVERSHAM— THOMAS STEPHENS — JOHN PHILLPOTT — ANDREW HEWETT, AND OTHERS	56
XVII. CANTERBURY— NICHOLAS SHETTERDEN—STEPHEN KEMPE THOMAS CRANMER	62
A PROPOSAL	79

LIST OF ILLUSTRATIONS

ROCHESTER CATHEDRAL	*Frontispiece*
	FACING PAGE
MARTYRS' MEMORIAL, OXFORD	16
MARTYRS' MEMORIAL, DARTFORD	24
MARTYR'S MEMORIAL, PEMBURY	32
MARTYRS' MEMORIAL, STAPLEHURST	44
WESTGATE, CANTERBURY	56
MARTYRS' MEMORIAL, CANTERBURY	64
CANTERBURY CATHEDRAL	72

NOBLE MARTYRS OF KENT

I

INTRODUCTORY

DOUBTLESS there have been other brave martyrs beside those for Protestantism. All are to be commended who have the courage to suffer for their convictions, not to say to give their lives for their principles.

We propose to deal especially with the Protestant Martyrs of Kent. Kent means "headland" or "corner," and it is truly the head of all the counties in the land for its number of martyrs in the Marian Persecution, for no fewer than sixty-four out of the three hundred or more victims of Popish error and victors for Protestant truth, in that eventful period, were from "The Garden of England." Most of these were done to death at Canterbury. Some forty-one were burnt to death in the Martyrs' Field, and five were starved to death in the Castle. The great majority were from outside that ecclesiastical city, and were brought from town and village to pass through their fiery trial.

The arms of Kent are very suggestive, namely, a white horse rampant, with the motto "Invicta," meaning unconquered or invincible. This word fittingly describes the spirit of those who, through the Conquering Christ of Calvary (and there is a vision of Him, and the white horse, in Rev. xix. 11), were enabled to say, " Nay, in all thése things we are more than conquerors through Him that loved us " (Rom. viii. 37).

Froude in his *History of England* (vol. vi. p. 101) with burning words thus describes the cruelty of Rome's representatives, Cardinal Pole and Queen Mary, and their willing servants : " They went out into the highways and hedges ; they gathered up the lame, the halt, the blind ; they took the weaver from his loom, the carpenter from his workshop, the husbandman from his plough ; they laid hands on maidens and boys. . . . Old men tottering to their grave, and children whose lips could but just lisp the articles of their creed, and of these they made their burnt-offerings ; with these they crowded their prisons, and when filth and famine killed them, they flung them out to rot."

Moreover, Lord Burghley said : " By imprisonment, by torment, by famine, by fire, almost the number of four hundred were in their various ways lamentably destroyed."

It is instructive and inspiring to think of lovely Kent, with its beauty and fertility so evident, as being the most fruitful of all the counties in producing fearless witnesses for the Protestant faith.

We propose a tour through Kent, visiting the spots made historic in Protestantism by God's faithful people. Our pilgrimage will commence at Rochester —famous for its Cathedral and Castle, famed also as Dickens-land, but honoured indeed through those linked to this ancient city on the Martyrs' Roll.

II

ROCHESTER

Nicholas Ridley

THE first martyr with whom we meet is Nicholas Ridley, who was Bishop of Rochester for two years and seven months. He was born in the county of Northumberland, being descended from a much-respected family. His early education was received at Newcastle. From thence he went to the University of Cambridge, where he soon became famous for his singular aptness for learning, and was called to high office in the University. Whilst head of Pembroke Hall he was made Doctor of Divinity.

Ridley travelled on the Continent for three years to increase his knowledge, and thus made the acquaintance of some of the early Reformers, whose doctrine he afterwards espoused. On his return to Cambridge, he was made Proctor of the University, and as such protested against the claims of the Pope to exercise ecclesiastical jurisdiction over the realm. He was chosen as Public Orator, and through the influence of Archbishop Cranmer was given the living of Herne, near Herne Bay. In the church there is to be seen a small memorial of him with the inscription: "In memory of Nicholas Ridley, Martyr, sometime Vicar of Herne. For the Word of God and the testimony of Jesus Christ." He became one of the Chaplains to King Henry VIII., and on September 4th, 1547, was elevated to the Bishopric of Rochester.

In April 1550, during the reign of Edward VI., he was promoted to the See of London. In his important offices he so diligently applied himself to the preaching and teaching of "the true and wholesome doctrine of Christ," that he was deeply beloved by his flock in both of his dioceses. He was truly anxious to gain the Papists from their erroneous opinions, and sought by gentleness to win them to the truth.

One incident will illustrate his godly zeal. Notwithstanding the changes in religion since the abolition of Papal supremacy in England, the daughter of Henry VIII., Princess Mary (afterwards Queen Mary), refused to conform to them, and maintained the service of the Mass. Bishop Ridley went to visit her at Hunsden, when there ensued the following curious dialogue, which we reproduce from John Foxe:

"After the Bishop had saluted the Princess, he said he had come to do his duty to her. Then she thanked him for his pains, and for a quarter of an hour talked with him very pleasantly, and said she knew him in the Court when he was chaplain to her father, and could well remember a sermon he had preached before King Henry, and so dismissed him to dine with her officers. After dinner, the

Bishop was called for by the Princess, and the conversation was as follows :

"BISHOP.—'Madam, I came not only to do my duty to see your Grace, but also to offer myself to preach before you on Sunday next, if it will please you to hear me.'

"At this her countenance changed, and after silence for a space, she answered thus :

"MARY.—'My lord, as for this matter, I pray you make the answer to it yourself.'

"BISHOP.—'Madam, considering mine office and calling, I am bound in duty to make to your Grace this offer, to preach before you.'

"MARY.—'Well, I pray you make the answer (as I have said) to this matter yourself; for you know the answer well enough. But if there be no remedy, I must make you answer: the door of the parish church adjoining shall be open for you, if you come, and you may preach if you list; but neither I nor any of mine shall hear you.'

"BISHOP.—'Madam, I trust you will not refuse God's Word.'

"MARY.—'I cannot tell what ye call God's Word; that is not God's Word now, that was God's Word in my father's days.'

"BISHOP.—'God's Word is one in all times, but hath been better understood and practised in some ages than in others.'

"MARY.—'You durst not, for your ears, have avouched that for God's Word in my father's days that now ye do. And as for your new books, I thank God I never read any of them; I never did, nor ever will do.'

"And after many bitter words against the form of religion then established, and against the government of the realm, and the laws made in the young years of her brother, Edward vi.—which she said she was not bound to obey till her brother came to perfect age, and then she affirmed she would obey them—she asked the Bishop whether he were one of the Council. He answered, ' No.' ' You might well enough be,' said she, ' as the Council goeth nowadays.'

"And so she concluded with these words : ' My lord, for your gentleness to come and see me, I thank you ; but for your offering to preach before me, I thank you not a whit.'

"After he had partaken of some refreshment in the place where he had dined, Ridley paused awhile, looking very sad, and suddenly broke out into these words : ' Surely I have done amiss, for I have drunk in the place where God's Word offered hath been refused ; whereas, if I had remembered my duty, I ought to have departed immediately, and to have shaken off the dust of my shoes for a testimony against this house.' These words were spoken with such vehemence that some of the hearers afterwards confessed their hair to stand upright on their heads ! This done, the Bishop departed, and so returned to his house."

Bishop Ridley was first brought to a knowledge of Christ by reading Bertram's book on *The Sacrament*, and his conference with Archbishop Cranmer and Peter Martyr did much to confirm him in that belief. Being now, by the grace of God, thoroughly converted to the true way, he was as constant and faithful in the right knowledge which the Lord had revealed to him, as he was before blind and zealous in his old ignorance of the Truth. He was mighty in his influence for spiritual good.

Alas! on Mary's accession to the throne he was one of the first upon whom the persecutors laid their hands and sent to prison—first in the Tower of London, and from thence conveyed to Oxford, and with Archbishop Cranmer and Bishop Latimer confined in the common prison of Bocardo; but being separated from them, he was committed to custody in the house of Mr. Irish, Mayor of Oxford, where he was kept till the day of his martyrdom, from 1554 until October 16th, 1555. He was cited, with Latimer, to appear before the Lords Commissioners at the Divinity School, Oxford.

Ridley was examined first, and afterwards Hugh Latimer, Bishop of Worcester. The Commissioners appointed by Cardinal Pole were: John White, Bishop of Lincoln; Dr. Brooks, Bishop of Gloucester; and Dr. Holyman, Bishop of Bristol. After a lengthy examination, in which both Ridley and Latimer gave fearless and faultless replies, Ridley confessed that at one time he held the doctrines of the Church of Rome, but he now rejected them entirely wherein they differed from the Bible. He was then requested to answer certain Articles drawn up by his episcopal judges.

"*Item* 1.—'We do object to thee, Nicholas Ridley, first that thou, in this high University of Oxford, in the year 1554, hast affirmed, and openly defended and maintained, and in many other times and places besides, that the true and natural body of Christ, after the consecration of the Priest, is not really present in the Sacrament of the Altar.'

"*Item* 2.—' That in the said year aforesaid thou hast publicly affirmed and defended that in the Sacrament of the Altar remaineth still the substance of bread and wine.'

"*Item* 3.—' That in the said year thou hast openly affirmed, and obstinately maintained, that in the Mass is no propitiatory Sacrifice for the quick and the dead.'

"*Item* 4.—' That in the year, place, and months aforesaid, these the aforesaid assertions solemnly had been condemned, by the scholastical censure of this school, as heretical and contrary to the Catholic faith, by Dr. Weston, prolocutor then of the Convocation House, as also of other learned men of both the Universities.'

"*Item* 5.—' That the premises be true and openly known by public fame, as well to them near at hand as also to them in distant places.'"

After the examination, the Bishop of Lincoln, President of the Commission, concluded in the following words:

"Master Ridley, I am sorry to see such stubbornness in you, that by no means you will be persuaded to acknowledge your errors, and receive the truth; but seeing it is so, because you will not suffer us to persist in the first, we must of necessity proceed to the other part of our commission. Therefore, I pray you, hearken to what I shall say."

And forthwith he read the sentence of condemnation, which was written in a long process; the substance of which was, that the said Nicholas

Ridley did affirm, maintain, and stubbornly defend certain opinions, assertions, and heresies, contrary to the Word of God and the received faith of the Catholic Church, and could by no means be turned from his heresies. They therefore condemned him as an obstinate heretic, and adjudged him presently, both by word and in deed, to be degraded from the degree of a Bishop, from the priesthood, and all the ecclesiastical orders; declaring him, moreover, to be no member of the Church, and, therefore, they committed him to the secular powers, of them to receive due punishment according to the temporal laws.

Dr. Ridley was committed as a prisoner to the Mayor, Mr. Irish, till he should suffer death as appointed.

On the night before Ridley suffered, as he sat at supper, at the house of Mr. Irish, his custodian, he invited his hostess, and the rest at the table, to his marriage: "For," said he, "to-morrow I must be married." And he was as merry as ever he had been before. And wishing his sister to be at his marriage, he asked his brother, who was at the table, whether he thought she could find it in her heart to be there, to which the latter answered: "Yes, I dare say, with all her heart"; at which he said he was glad to hear of her sincerity.

At this discourse Mrs. Irish, the Mayoress, wept, but Dr. Ridley comforted her, saying: "Oh, Mrs. Irish! you love me not, I see well enough; for in that you weep, it doth appear you will not be at my marriage, neither are content therewith. Indeed, you are not so much my friend as I thought you were. Be quiet yourself; though my breakfast shall be somewhat sharp, yet my supper will be more pleasant."

The place of execution chosen was on the north side of Oxford, in the ditch over against Balliol College. Dr. Ridley had on a black gown, furred and faced, such as he used to wear as Bishop. He walked to the stake between the Mayor and an Alderman. As he passed towards the Bocardo Prison, he looked up to where Dr. Cranmer lay, hoping to see him at the window, and to speak to him.

Dr. Cranmer was engaged in a disputation with a Spanish friar, Soto, and his fellows, so that he could not see him. But Cranmer looked after them, and devoutly prayed to God to strengthen the faith and patience of Ridley and Latimer in their last but painful passage.

Then, looking back, Dr. Ridley saw Latimer coming after, unto whom he said: "Oh, are you there?" "Yea," said Latimer, "have after, as fast as I can." So he followed a little way off, until they came to the stake.

Dr. Ridley, entering the place first, earnestly holding up both his hands, looked steadfastly toward heaven; then shortly after, seeing Latimer with a cheerful look, he ran to him and embraced him, saying: "Be of good heart, brother, for God will either assuage the fury of the flame, or else strengthen us to abide it."

He then went to the stake, and kneeling down, prayed with great fervour, while Latimer, following, kneeled also, and prayed with like earnestness.

After this, Dr. Smith began his sermon to them on these words : "And though I give my body to be burned and have not charity, it profiteth me nothing" (1 Cor. xiii. 3).

Strange that this panegyric on love should have been so prostituted on this occasion.

At the conclusion of the sermon, Ridley said to Latimer: "Will you answer or shall I?"

Latimer said : "Begin you first, I pray you."

"I will," said Ridley.

He then knelt, with Latimer, to Lord Williams, the Vice-Chancellor of Oxford, and said : "I beseech you, my lord, even for Christ's sake, that I may speak but two or three words." And while my lord bent his head to the Mayor and the other Commissioners, the bailiffs ran hastily to him, and with their hands stopped his mouth.

Dr. Marshal said : "Master Ridley, if you will revoke your erroneous opinions, you shall not only have liberty so to do, but also your life."

"Not otherwise?" said Ridley.

"No," answered Marshal; "therefore, if you will not do so, there is no remedy ; you must suffer your deserts."

"Well," said the martyr Bishop, "so long as the breath is in my body, I will never deny my Lord Christ and His known truth. God's will be done in me."

With that he rose, and said with a loud voice: "I commit our cause to Almighty God, who will indifferently judge all."

Then the smith took a chain of iron and placed it about their waists ; and as he was knocking in the staple, Ridley took the chain in his hand, and looking aside to the smith, said: "Good fellow, knock it hard, for the flesh will have its course."

They then brought a lighted faggot, and laid it at Ridley's feet; upon which Latimer said: "Be of good comfort, Master Ridley, and play the man! We shall this day light such a candle, by God's grace, in England, as I trust never shall be put out."

Ridley was the longer to suffer because the faggots were piled too high and so close to his body. He said: "Let the fire come to me, for I cannot burn." A bag of gunpowder was put on the flames, and he expired at last, saying: "Lord Jesus, receive my spirit!"

Thus died the good Nicholas Ridley, once Bishop of Rochester.

We shall here do well to recall the beautiful poem of Wordsworth on these two brave martyr-bishops:

LATIMER AND RIDLEY

How fast the Marian death-list is unrolled!
See Latimer and Ridley in the might
Of faith stand coupled for a common flight!
One (like those prophets whom God sent of old)
Transfigured, from this kindling hath foretold
A torch of inextinguishable light;
The other gains a confidence as bold;
And thus they foil their enemy's despite.
The penal instruments, the shows of crime,
Are glorified while this once-mitred pair
Of saintly friends, the "murtherer's chain partake,
Corded, and burning at the social stake";
Earth never witnessed object more sublime
In constancy, in fellowship more fair!

III

ROCHESTER (*Continued*)

NICHOLAS HALL—JOHN HARPOLE—JOAN BEACH

THREE other names have added lustre to the glory of the city of Rochester—Nicholas Hall, John Harpole, and Joan Beach.

Nicholas Hall was a bricklayer of Dartford, and was tried with Christopher Waid, a fellow-townsman, before the then Bishop of Rochester, Maurice Griffiths.

It was the common charge of heresy. Hall refused to call the Holy Catholic Church his Mother, because he found not this word in connection with the Church in Scripture, and he declared the Mass to be naught and abominable as used. Sentence of condemnation was passed, and he was appointed to be burnt. This " brick " of a bricklayer was burnt to death at Rochester, July 19th, 1555.

John Harpole was a citizen of St. Nicholas Parish, Rochester. Joan Beach was a widow, of Tonbridge. Both were examined by the Bishop of Rochester, and condemned because they did " affirm, maintain," and believe, contrary to the Mother Holy Catholic Church of Christ, that in the Blessed Sacrament of the Altar under the form of Bread and Wine there is NOT the "Very Body and Blood of Our Saviour in substance, but only a token and memorial thereof."

Joan Beach declared that "the Holy Catholic Church was not her Mother, but believed only the Father in Heaven to be her Father."

It was because John Harpole and Joan Beach (as well as many others in those bitter days) so realized the error of Transubstantiation and its dishonour of their Saviour and Lord, that they were ready to seal their testimony with their life-blood. Both were condemned to death in one sentence at the Bishop's Palace by Bishop Griffiths, into whose prison they had been cast. It is this Bishop of whom Fuller, in his *Church History*, says: "This Bishop played the tyrant."

Early in the morning of April 1st, 1556, John Harpole and Joan Beach were led out to die. They were both chained to the stake, and again and again they were urged to recant, but every time they refused. The torch was applied to the faggots, and soon the flames did their deadly work.

These two martyrs were faithful unto death, and went to receive the crown of life.

IV

STROOD

WILLIAM WOOD—JOHN PEMMELL—JOHN BAILEY

WE pause awhile at Strood, where three heroic men are worthy of remembrance by Protestants—William Wood, a baker; John Pemmell, a fisherman; and John Bailey, a glover.

All three were willing to die the martyr's death, and no thanks to Rome that they perished not in the flames.

William Wood, on October 19th, 1558, was charged before the Mayor of Rochester in St. Nicholas Church, with heresy concerning "the Real Presence." He was examined by the Chancellor of the Diocese (Dr. Kennal), and Dr. Chedsey, a Commissioner and a bitter Romanist. These two divines differed respecting the proper definition of the word "Transubstantiation" (meaning "a change into another substance," namely, that the bread and wine become the actual Body and Blood of Christ).

Each was so full of passion that first one and then the other bounced out of his judgment-seat in the Church, leaving the so-called heretic alone with the Mayor.

William Wood was allowed quietly to escape, thanks to the Mayor.

John Pemmell and John Bailey were both brought before the Bishop at his Palace. It is the same Bishop (Maurice Griffiths) who was the first to light the martyr fires in Queen Mary's reign.

These two Strood men were charged with "non-attendance at Church and neglect of the Mass." While the case was proceeding in the Palace yard, where a large sailcloth had been fixed up to screen the Bishop and his supporters from the sun, the wind sprang up, and with such force that it blew down the screen, and injured some of the judges. The Bishop hastily rose and dismissed the cases.

These two brave Johns of Strood were set at liberty, though they were willing to burn rather than turn.

So there were three champions of the faith in Strood, who " kept the bridge in the brave days of old."

Let us now journey on to Cooling, for at Cooling Castle there lived the first Protestant martyr of Kent, the good Lord Cobham. He was one of the Lollards, the followers of John Wycliffe.

Lord Cobham, formerly Sir John Oldcastle, was a knight of Herefordshire and married the heiress of Cowling—or Cooling—Castle, near Rochester. He sat in Parliament under the title of Lord Cobham, in the right of his wife's barony.

In youth, Lord Cobham was gay and wild, though clever and cultured, but through studying the

MARTYRS' MEMORIAL, OXFORD

[Facing page 16

writings of John Wycliffe and reading the Bible his heart was changed, and he was truly converted.

Dr. J. A. Wylie, the Protestant historian, says: "So now to the knightly virtues of bravery and honour were added the Christian graces of humility and purity." He had borne arms under Henry IV. in France, and Henry had set a great value on his military accomplishments. He was a close companion to Henry V., then Prince Henry; but when he became a Lollard, he had to pay the price of his faithfulness.

Lord Cobham made no secret of his Christian faith. He moved from his place in Parliament, as early as 1391, that: "It would be very commodious for England if the Pope's jurisdiction stopped at Calais, and did not cross the sea." Would there were more lords of such character to-day! It is said that so keen was he for the Word of God to be circulated, that he had copies of Wycliffe's Bible prepared for France, Spain, Portugal, Bohemia, and other lands beside.

Cooling Castle was thrown open to the Lollards, and became their headquarters whilst in the district. Often Lord Cobham might have been seen with his hand resting on his sword ready to defend these brave witnesses for Christ against the friars and priests. Archbishop Arundel and the Bishops became very bitter against him, so much so that, in convocation at St. Paul's in 1413, the Archbishop rose and called attention to the progress of Lollardism in the land, and pointed to Lord Cobham as the chief abettor of the Lollards. His lordship had a friend in the King, who did his best to stay the persecution until, alas ! he was over-persuaded by the Archbishop to allow the persecutors to proceed with their cruel work.

Lord Cobham was arrested, taken to the Tower of London, then brought before the Archbishop and others and examined. He answered fearlessly and faithfully—" Not the crucifix, but Christ "— and declared the Pope to be Antichrist. He was sent back to the Tower as a prisoner, but escaped to Wales, where he remained four years. The sum of one thousand marks was offered as reward for Lord Cobham, dead or alive. Lord Powis discovered his hiding-place, and for greed of gold betrayed him. Taken by his pursuers, he was roughly handled, and in a scuffle his leg was broken. He was removed on a horse litter to London, and once more placed in the Tower. Again and again he was urged to recant. A false report was spread abroad to the effect that he had recanted ; but, on the contrary, he reaffirmed his faith.

At last it was decided " to hang and burn him " at St. Giles-in-the-Fields, to which place he was dragged on a hurdle. The grand old man knelt and prayed for forgiveness for the sins of his godless youth, and pardon for his enemies. He urged the people to accept the Word of God, to beware of false teachers, and ever to be true to Christ. While life lasted in the flames, he praised God all the time. Friars and priests slandered his character, and alleged that he was a rogue.

Even Shakespeare believed the lying statements for a time and introduced him in *Henry IV.*, but afterwards scratched out " Oldcastle " and put the name "Falstaff" instead when he knew the real facts of the case. Shakespeare's mind evidently changed too, for he said: "Sir John Oldcastle died a martyr, and this is not the man." He was a valiant martyr, and a virtuous peer.

To Lord Cobham fell the unique honour of being the first of the English nobility to suffer martyrdom and die for the Protestant faith in the fair county of Kent.

V

DARTFORD

CHRISTOPHER WAID—NICHOLAS HALL—MARGERY POLLEY

IT was in June 1555 that Christopher Waid, a linen-weaver, and Nicholas Hall, a bricklayer, both of Dartford, were arrested because of their Protestant principles, and charged with heresy before the notorious Maurice Griffiths, Bishop of Rochester. The arms of this oft-mentioned Bishop consisted of a black dragon, and can be seen in the choir of Rochester Cathedral. Apart from its heraldic meaning, the dragon speaks for itself.

Both these good men were sentenced to be burnt; Christopher Waid was appointed to suffer his penalty on July 17th, but Nicholas Hall was not put to death until July 19th; and this took place at Rochester, as already stated.

Christopher Waid was taken early in the morning to the Brent, and into a gravel pit used for the execution of felons. Christopher Waid and one Margery Polley—a widow of Pembury, who had previously been condemned for heresy by the same episcopal judge, Griffiths—were in charge of the Sheriff, who had a large retinue.

Margery Polley said to Christopher Waid, on seeing in the distance the large crowd assembled to behold the burning: " You may rejoice to see such a company gathered to celebrate your marriage this day," and both martyrs sang a psalm. Margery Polley was kept in the town until the Sheriff's return from Waid's execution, and was conveyed the same day to Tonbridge to meet her fate there.

Christopher Waid was stripped of his clothes in an inn, and clad in a long white garment. He was then led to the stake, which he embraced. He set his back to be chained as required.

A pitch barrel having been placed near him, he was fastened to the stake. As soon as this was done, he looked up to heaven and, with a loud and cheerful voice, said: " Shew me a token for good, that they which hate me may see it, and be ashamed: because Thou, Lord, hast helped me " (Ps. lxxxvi. 17).

Near the stake was a mound and four posts on the top, covered round about like a pulpit. Into this place a friar went, book in hand. Christopher Waid, on seeing the friar, urged the people to " heed the Gospel and beware of the errors of Rome."

The Sheriff interrupted Waid by saying: " Be quiet, Waid, and die patiently."

Waid said: " I am quiet, thank God, and so trust to die." All the time the friar stood still, looking as if he would speak, but could not. At length he departed.

Faggots were then piled around the martyr, who, with his own hands, opened a space for his face to be seen, and for him to see others. His voice was heard again and again, saying: " Lord

Jesus, receive my soul!" Not a sign of impatience or cowardice was visible, and when he could no longer speak, he put his hands over his head and toward heaven.

So died Christopher Waid, well named Christopher, "the Christ-bearer." It is recorded that "divers fruiterers came with horse-loads of cherries and sold them to the many people who had come to witness the martyrdom," but, while there were those who found pleasure in such painful sights, we rejoice that fruit abides, and abounds to the memory of the sufferers in those sad and bad days.

Ere we leave Dartford we must climb the East Hill, and see the splendid Martyrs' Memorial standing in the historic Old Burial-Ground:

THE DARTFORD MARTYRS' MEMORIAL

On the front side we read:

1851
Erected
to the Memory of
CHRISTOPHER WAID
Linen Weaver of Dartford.
A PROTESTANT
who was Burned for his Faith
on Dartford Brent
July 19, 1555.

He repeated at the stake:

"SHEW SOME TOKEN UNTO ME FOR GOOD, THAT THEY WHICH HATE ME MAY SEE IT, AND BE ASHAMED: BECAUSE THOU, LORD, HAST HELPED ME, AND COMFORTED ME."

On the left side, the inscription continues:

>Other Dartford Martyrs were
>**NICHOLAS HALL, 1555.**
>**MARGERY POLLEY, 1555.**
>Rev. vi. 9, 10, 11.

"I saw under the altar the souls of them that were slain for the Word of God, and for the testimony which they held: and they cried with a loud voice, saying, How long, O Lord, holy and true, dost Thou not avenge our blood on them that dwell on the earth? And white robes were given unto every one of them; and it was said unto them, that they should rest yet for a little season, until their fellow-servants also and their brethren, that should be killed as they were, should be fulfilled."

On the right side are the words:

>THE
>NOBLE
>ARMY OF
>MARTYRS
>PRAISE
>THEE.

On the rear side of the Monument are the words:

>This
>**MARTYRS' MONUMENT**
>in the spirit of
>the Recorded
>Anointing
>of the Saviour
>with Costly Ointment
>is
>for a Memorial
>of Love
>to Jesus and His Church.

Around the base of the Monument are the words:

"Precious in the Sight of the Lord is the Death of His Saints."

On one of the sides is also the statement:

"This Monument was restored by Public Subscription, a.d. 1888."

MARTYRS' MEMORIAL, DARTFORD

[Photo by Snowdon Bros., Dartford] [Facing page 24

VI

SEVENOAKS

JOHN FRITH

THIS town received its name from seven large oak trees which stood upon the eminence where the town was afterwards built. The outstanding object of present interest, amid the beautiful woodland scenery of this delightful place, is the name of one of England's noblest "hearts of oak," as proved by his soundness, strength, and stability in his service and suffering for Christ's sake, namely, John Frith.

He was the son of an innkeeper, but, as John Foxe says: "He was possessed of marvellously quick parts, and with diligence and delight in learning equal to his genius, he would have opened for himself an easy road to honours and dignities had he not wholly consecrated himself to the service of the Church of Christ."

He commenced his studies at Cambridge, but was afterwards appointed by Cardinal Wolsey to serve with other learned scholars at his College at Oxford.

Frith first received the truth of the Gospel through another University student, William Tyndale, and these two saintly scholars "were perfectly emancipated from the yoke of the Papacy," and their emancipation had been accomplished by the Word of God alone. Soon the persecuting spirit of Rome began its evil work, and John Frith was committed to prison by Cardinal Wolsey with eight others from Wolsey's College. Their prison was "a damp and dark cellar below the buildings of the college, smelling rankly of the putrid articles stored up in it. Here these young doctors and scholars were left breathing the fetid air and enduring great misery."

Foxe gives even fuller details of this gloomy and gruesome place of incarceration. " A deep cave under the ground of the same college, where their salt fish was laid, so that through the filthy stench thereof they were all infected " (vol. v. p. 5).

After their examination they were condemned to do public penance for their "erroneous" opinions. A great fire was kindled in the market-place; the prisoners — than whom, of all the youth of Oxford, none had a finer genius, or were more accomplished in letters—were marshalled in procession; with faggot on shoulder they marched through the streets to where the bonfire blazed, and finished their penitential performance by throwing their heretical books into it.

After this, they were again sent back to their dungeon. For weeks Frith and his companions in tribulation were kept in their noisome prison; their strength ebbed away, and although they beguiled the time by prayer and helpful conversation, the chilly damp and corrupted air did their terrible work upon them. Four were allowed to depart, but only to die as the result of this callous treatment.

For six months they sustained life in this dreadful place, with poison in the air and fever in their blood, but they lived to serve the cause they so nobly represented. Some shone in the schools, others in the pulpit, and others, like Frith, consummated at the stake, long years after, the martyrdom they had begun in the dungeon at Oxford.

After many labours in the cause of Christ, Frith decided to assist William Tyndale in the translation of the New Testament, and so laboured that his fellow-countrymen might receive the light of the Gospel. On the completion of this glorious task, he felt compelled to return to England from Antwerp, whither he had gone to help his friend, Tyndale. He then began to preach the Gospel from house to house. He also used his pen with power, and to him belongs the honour of being the first to write against the Corporeal Presence in the Sacrament. His writings fell into the hands of Sir Thomas More, and were answered by him; but instead of being allowed to defend his faith, he was arrested, by the order of Sir Thomas More, on behalf of Cardinal Wolsey, and was once more put in prison. Then, though loaded with irons, and without books, he replied. For these offences he was taken before Bishops Stokesly, Gardiner, and Longland, his judges, in May 1533, when he bravely gave his reasons for the faith he held.

The Bishops seemed unwilling to condemn this scholar and saint, but he was so resolute in the stand he had taken that Stokesly pronounced sentence and delivered him to the secular power, " at the same time desiring that his punishment might be moderated, so that the rigour might not be too extreme, nor yet the gentleness of it too much mitigated "—a piece of hypocrisy which deceived no one.

Frith, with a fellow-martyr, one Andrew Hewitt, was brought to the stake at Smithfield on July 4th, 1533. On arriving there, he expressed great joy, and hugged the faggots with delight. A priest named Cook, who stood by, told the people not to pray for the culprits any more than they would do for a dog. At this, Frith smiled, and prayed God to forgive him. The fire was then kindled, and the martyrs consumed to ashes; but their names live still.

John Frith has left a name in Sevenoaks—aye, and in his native land!—that is writ large in deep, clear, and imperishable letters. He was the writer of some scholarly volumes on the Sacrament of the Lord's Supper and on Purgatory. He encountered many troubles, some of which he set forth in a Letter to his Friends, paragraphs from which are herewith reproduced:

"I doubt not, dear brethren, but that it doth some deal vex you, to see the one part to have all the words, and freely to speak what they list, and the others to be put to silence, and not be heard indifferently. But refer your matters unto God, who shortly shall judge after another fashion. In the meantime, I have written unto you, as briefly as I may, what articles were objected against me, and what were the principal points of my condemnation, that ye might understand the matter certainly.

" The whole matter of this my examination was comprehended in two special articles, that is to say, Of Purgatory, and Of the Substance of the Sacrament.

" And first of all, as touching Purgatory, they inquired of me whether I did believe there was any place to purge the spots and filth of the soul after this life ? But I said, that I thought there was no such place : for man (said I) doth consist and is made only of two parts, that is to say, of the body and the soul, whereof the one is purged here in this world, by the cross of Christ, which He layeth upon every child that He receiveth ; as affliction, worldly oppression, persecution, imprisonment, etc. The last of all, the reward of sin, which is death, is laid upon us : but the soul is purged with the Word of God, which we receive through faith, to the salvation both of body and soul. Now if ye can show me a third part of man besides the body and the soul, I will also grant unto you the third place, which ye do call Purgatory. But because ye cannot do this, I must also of necessity deny unto you the Bishop of Rome's Purgatory. Nevertheless, I count neither part a necessary article of our faith, to be believed under pain of damnation, whether there be such a Purgatory or no.

" Secondly, they examined me touching the Sacrament of the Altar, whether it was the very body of Christ or no ?

" I answered, that I thought it was both Christ's body and also our body, as St. Paul teacheth us in 1 Cor. x. For in that it is made one bread of many corns, it is called our body, which, being divers and many members, are associated and gathered together into one fellowship or body. Likewise of the wine which is gathered of many clusters of grapes, and is made into one liquor. But the same bread again, in that it is broken, is the body of Christ; declaring His body to be broken and delivered unto death, to redeem us from our iniquities.

"Furthermore, in that the sacrament is distributed, it is Christ's body signifying that as verily as the sacrament is distributed unto us, so verily are Christ's body and the fruit of His passion distributed unto all faithful people.

"In that it is received, it is Christ's body, signifying that as verily as the outward man receiveth the sacrament with his teeth and mouth, so verily doth the inward man, through faith, receive Christ's body and the fruit of His passion, and is as sure of it as of the bread which he eateth.

"Well (said they), dost thou not think that His very natural body, flesh, blood, and bone, is really contained under the sacrament, and there present without all figure or similitude? No (said I), I do not so think: notwithstanding I would not that any should count, that I make my saying (which is the negative) any article of faith. For even as I say, that you ought not to make any necessary article of the faith of your part (which is the affirmative), so I say again, that we make no necessary article of the faith of our part, but leave it indifferent for all men to judge therein, as God shall open their hearts; and no side to condemn or despise the other, but to nourish in all things brotherly love ; and one to bear another's infirmity.

. . . .

" As touching the cause why I cannot affirm the doctrine of Transubstantiation, divers reasons do lead me thereunto : first, for that I do plainly see it to be false and vain, and not to be grounded upon any reason, either of the Scriptures or of approved doctors. Secondly, for that by my example I would not be an author unto Christians to admit anything as a matter of faith, more than the necessary points of their creed, wherein the whole sum of our salvation doth consist, especially such things, the belief whereof hath no certain argument of authority or reason. I added, moreover, that their Church (as they call it) hath no such power and authority, that it either ought or may bind us, under the peril of our souls, to the believing of any such articles. Thirdly, because I will not, for the favour of our divines or priests, be prejudicial in this point unto so many nations, of Germans, Helvetians, and others, which altogether rejecting the transubstantiation of the bread and wine into the body and blood of Christ, are all of the same opinion that I am, as well those that take Luther's part as those that hold with Œcolampadius. Which things standing in this case, I suppose there is no man of any upright conscience, who will not allow the reason of my death, which I am put unto for this only cause, that I do not think transubstantiation, although it were true indeed, to be established for an article of faith."

VII

WROTHAM

JOHN CORNEFORD

WE will now go from the busy towns to the quiet village of Wrotham. Can any good thing come out of a village? Come and see; for out of the various places represented in Kent by Protestant Martyrs, are nine towns, but no fewer than nineteen villages. Brave victors of the village!

John Corneford, of Wrotham, was one of the last five burnt in the Marian Persecution. Queen Mary was very ill at the time, but so bitter against the Protestants that she would not wait for recovery; rather she wished the brutal work to continue. John Corneford, with others, was tried for rejecting the doctrines of Transubstantiation, and Prayers to the Virgin Mary and the Saints. This hero of the village was burnt at Canterbury on November 15th, 1558, and witnessed a good confession for Christ.

While at Wrotham we cannot but be impressed by its magnificent views. And it will be well worth our while at this quiet and charming spot to see that we have right conceptions concerning the dogma of Transubstantiation, since Rome so persistently made this the touchstone with which to

MARTYR'S MEMORIAL, PEMBURY

Photo by H. H. Camburn, Tunbridge Wells

test her many victims. This dogma was broached as early as the ninth century, but not formally established until the Council of Lateran, 1215, under Pope Innocent III.; nor was it till three centuries later that the Council of Trent decreed it to be " a true and propitiatory Sacrifice."

Canon I. of the Council of Trent (A.D. 1545–1563, Session XIII.) says : " If any shall deny that in the Sacrament of the most holy Eucharist, there is contained truly, really, and substantially the body and blood, together with the soul and divinity of our Lord Jesus Christ, but shall say that He is only in it in sign, or figure, or power, let him be accursed."

" It is also in this place to be explained by the pastors that there is contained, not only the true body of Christ, and whatever belongs to a true condition (or definition) of a body, such as Bones and Nerves, but also a whole Christ." Again, " It ought to be accounted but one and the same Sacrifice which is done in the Mass, and which was offered on the Cross " (*Catechism of Council of Trent*).

" This Council began its deliberations by repudiating the maxim of Protestants that Scripture is the final authority. At its third Session it decreed that the traditions of the Fathers are of equal authority with the Scriptures of the Old and New Testaments, and that no one is to presume to interpret Scripture in a sense different from that of the Church. This secured that nothing should emanate from the Council save a series of thoroughly Popish decisions and dogmas, all of them, like the first, under the pain of Anathema " (*History of Protestantism*, Dr. J. A. Wylie).

The Corpus Christi Festival of the Roman Catholic Church was instituted by Pope Urban, between 1262 and 1264, in honour of Transubstantiation. It is celebrated on the Thursday after Trinity Sunday. The Corpus Christi Procession is illegal in England as declared in the Roman Catholic Emancipation Act (Sec. 26, 10 George IV., c. 7, 1829). "And be it further enacted that if any Roman Catholic ecclesiastic, or any member of any of the Orders, Communities, or Societies hereinafter mentioned, shall, after the commencement of this Act, exercise any of the Rites or Ceremonies of the Roman Catholic Religion, or wear the Habits of his Orders save within the usual places of Worship of the Roman Catholic Religion or in private houses, such ecclesiastic or other person shall, being thereof convicted by the course of law, forfeit for every such offence the sum of fifty pounds." This Act, while giving certain rights to Roman Catholics, expressly provided that no objects or symbols of worship should be brought into the public street.

Such legislation became necessary owing to the tyranny and persecution of the Church of Rome when in the past she held sway in England. And since she is unchanged at heart (and even boasts of her unchangeableness), we need to guard well our liberties, because the same spirit still prevails wherever she has predominance, as seen where the Corpus Christi Procession is carried on, and as proved by the bitter experience of Protestants even now in such Roman Catholic countries as Italy, Spain, South America, and even the South of Ireland.

And this very Act goes to make pure the liberties we all enjoy, whether Protestant or Roman Catholic.

The claim of the Church of Rome in their dogma of Transubstantiation to offer the Sacrifice of the Mass and repeat the Sacrifice of Christ offered for our sins at Calvary, is a grave reflection on the efficacy of His atoning death, for it implies that the work of Christ on our behalf is incomplete ; whereas Christ Himself declared in His dying words on the Cross, " It is finished " (John xix. 30). It is deplorably unscriptural, for no less than seven times in relation to Christ's Death as our Substitute, do we find the truth expressed thus, " Once," " Once offered," " Once for all," " One sacrifice for sins for ever " (Heb. vii. 27 ; ix. 12, 26, 28 ; x. 10, 12, 14 ; and in six of these references the same word is used, meaning " Once for all "). It is worthy of notice in these days, that the Church of England, in her Catechism and Thirty-nine Articles, speaks on this matter with no uncertain sound.

In the Catechism there is the *Question* (*re* the Sacraments) : " Why was the Sacrament of the Lord's Supper ordained ? "

Answer : " For the continual remembrance of the Sacrifice of the Death of Christ, and the benefits which we receive thereby."

In the Articles we read :

" ARTICLE 28.—Transubstantiation (or the change of the Substance of Bread and Wine) in the Supper of the Lord cannot be proved by Holy Writ ; but is repugnant to the plain words of Scripture, overthroweth the nature of a Sacrament, and hath given occasion to many superstitions."

"ARTICLE 31.—*Of the one Oblation of Christ finished upon the Cross.*—The Offering of Christ once made is that perfect redemption, propitiation, and satisfaction for all the sins of the whole world, both original and actual; and there is none other sacrifice for sin, but that alone. Wherefore the *Sacrifices of Masses*, in the which it was commonly said that the Priest did offer Christ for the quick and the dead, to have remission of pain or guilt, were blasphemous fables and dangerous deceits."

While thinking and talking so much about this false doctrine of Transubstantiation, it should mean to us something far more than a mere matter of opinion, or theological discussion, or even Church History. Do we realize the fact that "Christ died for *us*" (Rom. v. 8); that "Christ died for our sins according to the Scriptures" (1 Cor. xv. 3)? Can we truly say: "He loved me, and gave Himself for me" (Gal. ii. 20)?

Now we are on this pilgrimage together, let us settle the question by trusting Christ as our own personal Saviour. Then can we rejoice that no repetition of Christ's Sacrifice for Sin is required, but rather it is our gracious privilege to celebrate the Lord's Supper as a "Remembrance Feast," whilst obeying His word: "This do in remembrance of Me" (Luke xxii. 19). For as it is so well put in the chorus of the hymn, written and sung by that sweet singer of the Gospel, the late P. P. Bliss:

> "Once for all, O sinner, receive it;
> Once for all, O brother, believe it;
> Cling to the Cross, thy burden shall fall—
> Christ hath redeemed us, once for all."

As Protestants we protest against the grievous error of Transubstantiation, for it deprives Christ of His glory as Saviour, it dishonours the Sacred Word, it degrades the Sacrament of the Lord's Supper by making it idolatrous, it deludes the soul concerning Salvation, and delights the Evil One by doing his work of deception. "Protestant" means "One who testifies for or before"; it is therefore not only negative, but also very positive. Let us stand boldly against this, and all the other errors of Rome, and fearlessly testify on behalf of the finished work of Christ—a complete Salvation, a perfect Redemption, wrought out for us by Jesus our Saviour on the Cross.

The word "martyr" reproduces a Greek word meaning "a witness"; and the witnesses of Christ, known as martyrs, sealed their testimony with their blood. Although we may not be called upon to give our lives for the Christian faith, we can be witnesses in our respective spheres through the power of the Holy Spirit (Acts i. 8), and give clear evidence of what we have seen, heard, and experienced of the Salvation of Christ, our Substitute-Saviour, received by simple faith as a free gift (Rom. v. 1; vi. 23). We thus bear our witness without any unkind feeling toward Roman Catholics as such, for we have among them friends whose character and devotion we greatly admire. Our opposition is to the terrible system that holds them, and the woeful heresies by which they are enthralled.

After this somewhat lengthy conversation in this restful village, made famous by one of its former inhabitants, the lone but loyal martyr, John Corneford, let us now pass on.

VIII

MAIDSTONE

Edward Walker—Thomas Hitton—John Denley—John Newman, and Others

NO fewer than thirteen names were added to the scroll of fame at Maidstone. Twelve were burnt to death and one died in prison.

The first martyrdom connected with this town took place on May 2nd, 1511, when Edward Walker was consumed in the flames because he was true to the Divine Word and his Divine Lord.

The second was in March 1530, when Rev. Thomas Hitton was burnt near the door of his own parish church. Tyndale speaks of him in his writings as "a preacher of Christ's Gospel whom the Bishop of Rochester and the Archbishop of Canterbury bitterly persecuted, on account of his Evangelical ministry, and at last had him burnt to death."

The third martyr connected with Maidstone was John Denley, who was burnt at Uxbridge on August 8th, 1555.

The fourth was William Minge, who died in prison at Maidstone on July 2nd, 1555. He was as truly a martyr as any who went to the stake.

The fifth case was that of John Newman, of

Maidstone, a pewterer, who was burnt at Saffron Walden, August 31st, 1555.

The sixth instance was that of Christopher Browne, who gave his life at the stake at Canterbury, November 15th, 1555.

The seventh must be noticed more fully. There were seven in all in this company, and all were burnt in the King's Meadow, or Fairfield.

Edmund Allen and his wife Catherine. Allen was a miller of Frittenden, and had sold his corn more cheaply than others in order to benefit the poor; he had also given them the Bread of Life.

Walter Appleby, and Petronil his wife, were both natives of Maidstone, and lived quite near the Martyrs' Field, so they died for Christ's sake close to their own home. Peculiar pathos is added to this when, as we know, young children were left behind to mourn their loss.

Joan Bradbridge and Mrs. Manning, two brave women; and last of all, Elizabeth Lewis, a blind orphan maiden.

These seven were lodged in the old gaol at the top of the High Street. As they came forth from the prison, and Elizabeth was groping her way, the Sheriff roughly said, "What ails thee, maiden?" The people answered: "Your worship, Elizabeth is blind." It was on Friday, June 18th, 1555, these seven were chained to the stake and burnt to ashes, because of their faithful testimony; and blind Elizabeth, like the rest, went through fire to "see the King in His beauty," and receive at His hands the martyr's crown.

Before leaving Maidstone, we shall do well to

visit the Museum, and read the beautiful poem by the late Rev. H. H. Dobney, on "The Martyred Seven." We shall certainly be touched and thrilled by this epic of Christian constancy and courage.

THE MARTYRED SEVEN

The summer sun was shining o'er our fair fields of Kent,
When down our wondering High Street a strange procession went ;
It came not from the palace, it came not forth from hall,
Nor from the bridal dwelling, where merry bells ring all.

No troop of gallant horsemen, was neither squire nor knight ;
No noble's wrist held falcon all ready for the flight.
There was no sound of laughter, no merry music there,
But hushed the people's voices and silent all the air.

And faces at the windows were ghastly pale that day ;
And mothers clasped their little ones, and tried, dear hearts, to pray ;
And strong men muttered curses, and slow drew in their breath,
For the seven that were passing, were passing to their death.

Not by the sharp sword's swiftness, nor by the axe's blow,
But they must yield their bodies to death by torture slow ;
For the massive stake is driven, and the faggots piled around,
And the rough, unpitying doomsman is ready on the ground.

So the prison doors have opened and yielded forth the seven,
Dazed by the sudden sunshine and the bright blue of the heaven ;
For the jailer to the Sheriff has given his prisoners o'er,
And, roughly ordered, on they move, the javelin men before.

One was a yeoman sturdy, his pale wife by his side ;
Did there flash on Allen's mem'ry the day she was his bride?
And a second loving couple are walking in their rear,
Their rifled home close by—where are their children dear.

And then two others follow to witness in the flame,
How dear to them the Gospel, how dear their Saviour's Name ;
And still another doomed one, the crowd with wonder see,
For naught is known about her, save that an orphan maiden she ;

And only eighteen summers have bloomed upon the maid,
Yet for her, so young and tender, Rome's faggots, too, are laid.
And must she yield her body to the cruel, torturing flame ?
Aye, and she'll yield it gladly for love of Jesus' name.

But see, she gropes and falters, feebly holds forth her hand,
And feels for one to lead her, else she can hardly stand :
What ails the maiden ? roughly the Sheriff seeks to find ;
They answer him, "Your worship, Elizabeth is blind."

And now they've reached the meadow, now they're fastened to the stake,
The wood and furze piled round them, their last look let them take
On tree and sky and river and faces that they know,
For come is the dread moment, and now the red flames glow.

O Jesus, Thou art faithful, Thou know'st how sharp death's sting,
Be with Thy loyal, loving ones, within that fiery ring :
I see, I see heaven's portals, wide opening at Thy word,
And now, e'en now, Thy martyred ones are safely with their Lord.

And now, ye men of England, how love ye Gospel truth ?
How prize ye now the freedom, bought with so much of ruth ?
What lives are yours, my masters ? Whose followers are ye ?
If Truth to-day wants martyrs, will ye Truth's martyrs be ?

IX

TONBRIDGE

Joan Beach—Margery Polley

TONBRIDGE is noted for its splendid school, and is also famous for its connection with the national game of Cricket; but we are more interested to learn of some who here played victoriously in the great game of Life.

Two names claim our attention and admiration, namely, those of Joan Beach and Margery Polley. Both have previously been mentioned, the former in connection with Rochester, and the latter with Dartford.

Margery Polley, widow, of Pembury, after being tried before the Bishop of Rochester, and "in high swelling style" (John Foxe), was condemned to be burnt. The Sheriff conveyed her to Tonbridge for the burning, *via* Dartford, after accompanying Christopher Waid on his way to death by fire at Dartford. She greatly heartened this man of God for his passing through the flames. At Tonbridge she herself bravely sealed her own confession of Christ with her life-blood.

Joan Beach, widow, of Tonbridge, was condemned to the stake by the same bigoted Bishop, and was burnt in the Cathedral city of Rochester the following year—April 1st, 1556. Those two faithful widows have left behind them undying names, and their heroic example should stir others to be steadfast and unmovable, whatever the cost.

While we are so near Pembury, the native place of Margery Polley, the bereaved wife of Richard Polley of Pembury, we must look in upon the pretty village, made memorable by the noble steadfastness of this godly woman to her Protestant convictions. Here we find, with pleasure, a most useful and durable monument erected to her memory, in the form of a grey granite drinking-fountain, with a trough for horses and cattle, and a smaller one underneath for dogs. It stands on the side of the Hastings Road, and at the top of the upper green of the village.

This memorial was so placed by the generosity of local and loyal Protestants. Thus the memory of Margery Polley, the first of the women martyrs of Kent in the Marian Persecution, is kept fresh in the minds of people to-day, by the perpetual service rendered in quenching the thirst of both man and beast. Nor are the children of the village unmindful of its purpose, for it not only refreshes them while at their games, but causes them to think of this solitary and splendid heroine who, for the Truth, passed through the flames to her rest and reward. On the front of the Memorial is the inscription:

To the Memory of MARGERY POLLEY of Pembury who suffered martyrdom at TONBRIDGE A.D. 1555
Erected by Voluntary Subscription.

On the back are the words, in large letters, and cut deeply like the rest, so that all may read and remember :

**"While we were yet sinners Christ died for us."—
(Romans v. 8.)**

So the Gospel, dearly loved by Margery of Pembury, is silently preached day by day, and the atoning work of her Saviour is proclaimed, year in, year out. Her testimony is therefore living and lasting, and without doubt will lead others also to think of and trust in her Saviour.

MARTYRS' MEMORIAL, STAPLEHURST

X

STAPLEHURST

Alice Potkins—Joan Bradbridge—Alice Benden

LET us now ramble through the Weald of Kent. Our first stop shall be Staplehurst, where we shall see the fine monument erected to the memory of three heroic women of Staplehurst, Alice Potkins, Joan Bradbridge, and Alice Benden.

> "Their faith and patience, love and zeal,
> Should make their memory dear."

Alice Potkins was a married woman, and was the first of these three heroines to suffer. She was examined at the same time as William Foster (of Stone), who told his judge that he "did not believe in praying to saints, nor yet in purgatory . . . and as to carrying a cross, he should as soon carry about a gallows on which his father had been hanged." Alice Potkins said she agreed with all that William Foster had said, and added: "I am resolved never to confess to a priest, nor to pray to a saint, nor creep to the cross."

When asked her age, Alice said: "I am forty-nine years according to my old life, but since I learned Christ, and believed in Him, I am only one year old." She was imprisoned in Canterbury Castle, October 14th, 1556, and before the year ended she died of starvation, with four others, and their bodies were buried in the highway.

Joan Bradbridge, a young unmarried woman, was also true to her trust. She was taken from Staplehurst to Maidstone, and there burnt to death. (She was one of the seven already mentioned, who gave their lives for Christ amid the flames in the King's Meadow.)

Alice Benden was the wife of Edward Benden of Staplehurst, a wicked man and a cruel husband. She refused to go to church, and on being asked why, she replied that she "could not go with a good conscience, because there was much idolatry committed against the glory of God." The poor woman was arrested and kept in prison for fourteen days, and then released for a while. Her husband tried to get her to go to church, but she refused. He then told the neighbours, and this led to her being put in prison a second time. Her cruel husband actually offered to pay the cost of her conveyance to prison. She gave herself up to avoid this additional suffering and humiliation. She was brought before Justice Roberts (of Cranbrook) and then was sent to Canterbury. Here she was examined by the Bishop of Dover, and condemned to prison and the stake. By order of this Bishop, she was put into a prison called "Monday's Hole," a small vault underground, where she had to lie on straw, between the city stocks and a stone wall, and there she remained without being permitted to

STAPLEHURST 47

change her attire for nine long weeks. Because she sang, she was removed to Westgate Prison, then taken to Canterbury Castle, whence she was led, with six others, to the Martyrs' Field. There this woman, betrayed by her husband, went home in a chariot of fire, rejoicing in her Saviour; and although suffering untold agony, she experienced unspeakable joy.

The Martyrs' Memorial at Staplehurst stands boldly at the cross-roads, and speaks to every passer-by. It is built of solid Aberdeen granite, and on it has been placed a decorative bronze tablet with the following inscription:

THE NOBLE ARMY OF MARTYRS PRAISE THEE.

This Monument is dedicated to the Memory of
ALICE POTKINS, JOAN BRADBRIDGE, and
ALICE BENDEN of Staplehurst,
also of EDMUND ALLEN and his WIFE,
who for the faith suffered death, 1556-1557,
during the Marian Persecution.

"We shall by God's grace light such a
candle in England as shall never be put out."

Erected 1904 by Protestants of Staplehurst and District.

"Thy Word is Truth."

Other places in the country honoured by being linked with martyrs, where no memorial exists as yet, might do well to follow the example of Staplehurst.

XI

SMARDEN

Agnes Snoth—Anne Albright—Joan Sole—Joan Catmer—John Lomas

AT Smarden, a Baptist widow, Agnes Snoth, has left an undying name and fame for the honour of her Lord. She was one of eighteen females who bravely suffered even unto death for Christ's sake in Kent. Wives and widows, women of tender youth and women of many years, were alike " faithful unto death."

Agnes Snoth at her trial refused to confess to a priest. She quoted Jas. v. 16: "Confess your faults one to another." She would confess as one to another, but not for Absolution. She rejected the Mass and Penance. Her sentence was that she " be handed over to the Sheriff to be burnt to death."

She went to her rest through fire, January 31st, 1556, with four others—Anne Albright, Joan Sole, Joan Catmer (widow), and a man named John Lomas—at Canterbury.

She declared herself to the very last " a witness of Christ and His truth," and sang psalms at the stake. The good knight, Sir John Norton, being present, wept much at the sad sight. So her sufferings were not in vain even then, and her influence still abides at Smarden.

XII

BIDDENDEN

William Waterer—Thomas Stephens

WE now go to Biddenden, for there are things for which this village is famed beside the Biddenden maids and cakes. Of course there is the tradition of the celebrated twin maids, who, joined in life, remained together in death. When they were born they were united at the hips and shoulders, and lived thus for thirty-four years. One was taken ill and died, but the other refused to be separated and expired six hours afterward. By their will they left certain land, the proceeds of which provide for loaves of bread, pieces of cheese, and curious cakes to be distributed at Easter.

Two martyrs were produced in this quaint and quiet spot—William Waterer, burnt at Canterbury, January 15th, 1557, and Thomas Stephens, burnt to death at Wye, January 16th, 1557.

Those two days are made memorable in the calendar of Biddenden, for on these particular days the Biddenden braves made history, and caused this village to be remembered for their courageous stand for Christ.

XIII

CRANBROOK

John Archer—William Lowick

THIS place was noted in the old days as the centre of the cloth industry. It was the policy of Edward III. to limit certain manufacturing establishments to particular counties. Kent was selected for the manufacture of broadcloth, and Cranbrook became the chief market-town for " the strong and durable broadcloths of good mixtures and colours " for which the Weald of Kent acquired a wide reputation. Cloth workers from every land came here to live at the King's charges until they were able to support themselves. Hence Cranbrook held a prominent position in the industrial and commercial life of Kent, but no longer is this so, for the manufacture of cloth is now carried on elsewhere (*History of the Weald of Kent*, Robt. Furley).

Cranbrook remains quiet and dignified with the memory of its past glory.

Of far more interest to us is the part played by two of Cranbrook's native sons, who have woven into the history of Kent a beautiful and lasting pattern of Christian heroism.

These champions for Christ were John Archer,

who was starved to death in Canterbury Prison, and William Lowick, who was burnt to death at Canterbury, January 15th, 1557.

During Queen Mary's reign there lived at Cranbrook, Sir John Baker, a notorious agent of persecution for the Church of Rome. He haled many to prison, and these two Cranbrook men had to face him. A chamber in the south porch of Cranbrook Church is called "Baker's Prison," for it was here that this petty tyrant kept the Protestants in custody. Honour be to John Archer, who preferred to starve rather than stifle his conscience, and to William Lowick, who would burn rather than turn.

XIV

TENTERDEN

John Waddon—William Carder—Agnes Grebil—John Lomas, and Others

THIS old town is celebrated for its steeple, which is so frequently used to suggest the illogical. The saying is that " Tenterden steeple was the cause of the Goodwin Sands."

There may be some connection, but it is evidently very remote. There is no doubt, however, about Tenterden's place in Protestant history.

Tenterden steeple is quite a landmark, and was used as a beacon tower to warn the people of the approach of the Spanish Armada to England's shores. Yet not a steeple, but the heroic stand of nine Protestants of Tenterden, who shine as stars even now, is our chief concern at this time.

John Waddon, of Tenterden, a priest who became a Lollard in the reign of Henry VI., was put in prison at Norwich Castle and was ultimately burnt to death in September 1428, because he believed God alone could forgive sins, and God alone was to be worshipped and not images.

William Carder and Agnes Grebil, natives of Tenterden, were burnt on May 2nd, 1511, in the reign of Henry VIII. The case of Agnes Grebil was sad indeed, because her own husband and her two sons betrayed her to the enemy. She was dragged through the streets of the town, and at last burnt to death.

John Lomas, a weaver of Huguenot descent, was tried again and again for heresy, and, since he would not yield, he was burnt at Canterbury, January 31st, 1556.

John Phillpott, Matthew Bradbridge, and Nicholas Final, three courageous men of Tenterden, were imprisoned at Canterbury because of their stand for the truth. After being nearly starved to death, they were burnt, the first at Wye and the others at Ashford.

The widow of Bradbridge and the widow of Final were taken to prison after this fierce trial in the loss of their husbands, and both were burnt at Canterbury. Widow Bradbridge asked the Bishop who condemned her to the stake if he would take and keep her two fatherless children when she was gone. The Bishop displayed his patience and charity by saying: " By the faith of my body, I will meddle with neither of them." Notwithstanding all these influences, she was faithful to the very last.

Tenterden merits a continuance of honourable record in the annals of Protestantism.

XV

ASHFORD AND HYTHE

JOHN BROWN—MATTHEW BRADBRIDGE—
NICHOLAS FINAL

FIVE martyrs were burnt at Canterbury, namely, Rev. Humphrey Middleton (Baptist minister), John Herst, Richard Collier, Richard Wright, and William Steere. But there is the dust of martyrs at Ashford itself, for three were burnt there.

John Brown, a townsman of Ashford, was travelling on a Gravesend barge and happened to sit close to a priest. The priest asked him: "Dost thou know who I am? Thou sittest near me, thou sittest on my clothes."

J. B.—" No, sir, I know not what you are."

PRIEST.—"I tell thee I am a priest, I sing for souls."

J. B.—" I pray you, sir, where find you the soul when you go to Mass?"

PRIEST.—" I cannot tell thee."

J. B.—" Then if you cannot tell me, how can you save the soul?"

PRIEST.—" Go thy way, thou heretic! I will be even with thee."

As soon as they landed, the priest put his threat into action. He went to the Archbishop of Canterbury (Warham), and informed against his interlocutor as

ASHFORD AND HYTHE

a heretic. A day or two later, John Brown was seized, tied to his own horse and taken to Canterbury, his wife and friends not knowing what had happened to him. For forty days he was kept in prison, and cruelly treated. His bare feet were placed on burning coals in a vain endeavour to make him recant. At last he was sent back to Ashford to be burned.

All this time his anxious wife had no knowledge of his whereabouts or circumstances. But later she heard that he was in Ashford; and finding that Brown had been put in the stocks, she stayed the whole night, cheering him and being cheered by him. His martyrdom took place on Whitsunday evening, 1517, but not before he had exhorted his wife to bring up the children in the fear of God.

Matthew Bradbridge and Nicholas Final, both of Tenterden, after having been all but done to death by starvation at Canterbury, were taken to Ashford to die at the stake, and their burning took place on January 16th, 1556.

We now pass on to Hythe, one of the Cinque Ports to the west of Folkestone. In the crypt of its ancient church may be seen a large number of human bones, said to be those of Britons and Saxons slain in a battle here in the year 456.

But we are more interested in the fate of the four brave natives who were slain for the faith and suffered martyrdom at Canterbury. George Catmer and Robert Streater were burnt on September 6th, 1555; Joan Catmer (widow of George Catmer), on January 31st, 1556; and William Hay, on January 15th, 1557; and their names are all to be found on the Memorial there.

XVI

WYE AND FAVERSHAM

Thomas Stephens—John Phillpott—Andrew Hewett, and Others

WYE was a town of much importance in olden days. It is now better known for its modern institutions, the Agricultural College and the racecourse. While rejoicing in the valuable work of the former and regretting the vicious influence of the latter, our special interest is in the spot where two brave martyrs, Thomas Stephens, of Biddenden, and John Phillpott, of Tenterden, nobly gave their lives at the stake on January 16th, 1557.

These heroic souls made history that day in Wye, in thus dying to prove their love and loyalty to Christ their Saviour and King.

While on the way to Faversham we pass through a further stretch of characteristic Kentish scenery, with its graceful variety and peaceful beauty, consisting of cornfields and fruit orchards, hop gardens and woodlands, green pastures and homely farmsteads. And thus travelling, we may profitably refer to some other of the places associated with the martyrs, but as yet unmentioned by us,

WESTGATE, CANTERBURY

Photo by R. & H. Fisk-Moore, Canterbury

Facing page 56

WYE AND FAVERSHAM

namely, Broomfield, Challoch, Stone, Horton, Sellinge, Brenchley, Halden, Thurnham, Rolvenden, Adisham.

The two villages last named claim special attention, for their respective vicars, John Frankesh and John Bland, made a bold defence of the truth and suffered a brave death at the stake for their Saviour's sake.

John Bland, Vicar of Adisham, was brought before his judges again and again, and each time witnessed a good confession. An able scholar and a firm believer in the Protestant faith, he faithfully discharged his pastoral duties, and was a man whose whole life was devoted to his fellows, as may be gathered from the following fact.

After entering the ministry of the Church of God, he was inflamed with a keen desire to profit his congregation. Twice he was cast into prison for preaching the Gospel, to be delivered through the intercession of his friends, yet he would preach again, as soon as he was at liberty, whereupon, being apprehended the third time, his friends would again have rescued him, if he had promised to abstain from preaching: he would give no such undertaking, repeating the words of the Apostle Paul (Rom. viii. 35): "Who shall separate us from the love of Christ? Shall tribulation, or distress, or persecution, or famine, or nakedness, or peril, or sword?"

He was bitterly persecuted at Adisham by the hirelings of the Roman Catholic authorities. Quietly he went on with his work during the early part of Queen Mary's reign, but on

September 24th, 1554, trouble began through John Austen, one of three brothers, all tools of Rome, who disturbed the service at the parish church, by casting aside the Lord's Table. On November 26th, the other two brothers, Richard and Thomas, charged the Vicar with using profane language concerning the Mass.

"If that be so," replied the Vicar, "then, God helping me, I will stand to the proof of it."

"Well," said his accusers, "we will have the Mass here next Sunday, and a preacher who will prove thee a heretic."

Thus it came about that John Bland was arrested in his own parish church, because he protested against this priest celebrating the Mass in the church of which he was Vicar. He was roughly and cruelly handled, and conveyed as a heretic to Canterbury, there to be imprisoned in the Castle. Later, he was removed to Ashford, and examined by the Archdeacon of Canterbury (Nicholas Harpsfield) in the house of the Bishop of Dover (Richard Thornden).

Soon after, he was brought before the notorious Sir John Baker (at Cranbrook), who, after bullying the prisoner, said at the close of his examination: "I will give six faggots to burn thee, ere thou should be unburned. Hence, knave! Hence!" He was thereupon taken to Maidstone Gaol and, after being held in "durance vile" for several months, was ultimately sent back to Canterbury Prison. At his last trial he had to appear before the Bishop of Dover, the Commissary (Robert Collins), appointed by the Cardinal and the Archdeacon of Canterbury. The examination by the Commissary was as follows :

COLLINS.—" Mr. Bland, you know that you are presented to us as one suspected of heresy. How say you ? Are you contented to conform yourself to the laws of this realm and of the holy Church ? "

BLAND.—" I deny that I am justly suspected of heresy."

COLLINS.—" You were brought before the Archdeacon and me, and matter of heresy laid to your charge."

BLAND.—" That matter was done and said a whole year ago, for I have been in prison this year and more. If you have anything against me by law, I desire that you let me know the law and matter, and I will answer according to the law."

Then said my lord Suffragan, the Bishop of Dover : " But that I am one of the judges, I would rise and stand by thee, and accuse thee to be a sacramentary ; and bring witness to prove it ; yea, and further, that thou hast called the Mass an abominable idol."

BLAND.—" You, my lord, never heard me say so ; but I heard you once say that, in your conscience you had abhorred the Mass three years."

COLLINS.—" Thou liest ; this is but a drift. You had better answer now else you shall go to prison again, and be called on Monday, and have articles laid to you ; and if you answer not them directly, you shall be condemned as a heretic, and that will be worse for you."

BLAND.—" Sir, I do not now, nor will then, deny to answer anything that you can lay to my charge by law; wherefore I trust you will let me have the benefit of the law."

COLLINS.—" Well, on Monday, at nine o'clock, you shall see the law and have the articles laid unto you."

After some conversation, the Bishop of Dover cried: " No more! I command you to hold your peace. Have him away, and bring in another."

That was the bitter spirit and brutal manner of those cruel men: " Have him away, bring in another!"

On Monday, June 13th, John Bland was again brought before the Bishop of Dover, the Papal Commissary, and the Archdeacon of Canterbury, three men under whom a great many were cruelly treated and barbarously slain at Canterbury, and among these, Rev. John Bland was first. On the 25th of the same month he appeared again at the Chapter-House, and there boldly withstood the authority of the Pope, whereupon he was condemned to death by the Bishop of Dover, and delivered to the secular power, to be burnt to death at Canterbury on July 12th, 1555, with his fellow-prisoners, John Frankesh, Humphrey Middleton, and Nicholas Shetterden.

And now we reach Faversham, where a young man named Andrew Hewett, a native of the town, twenty-four years of age, claims attention. Faversham is noted for explosives, cement, and beer, but, to us, especially for the brave young Protestant hero in the time of Henry VIII.

Hewett was a tailor's apprentice in London, his master being a Mr. Warren (of Watling Street).

WYE AND FAVERSHAM   61

Another young tailor named William Holt met Andrew Hewett, and suspecting that he was "a Gospeller," informed the Bishop of London (Stokesly). Officers were sent to arrest Andrew Hewett, who was put in irons and imprisoned in the Bishop's house. A kind friend took a file and cut the chain and Hewett escaped, only to be soon recaptured.

After a long and cruel imprisonment he was tried, with John Frith (of Sevenoaks). When asked concerning " the Real Presence " at his trial, Hewett said : " I think as John Frith."

The Bishop asked : " Is not the bread the real Body of Christ ? " Hewett replied : " I do not believe it." The Bishop smiled and said : " Why, John Frith is a heretic and condemned to be burnt." Hewett bravely answered : " I am content to go to prison to John Frith."

The two friends were burnt at Smithfield on the afternoon of July 4th, 1533.

Though young, away from home, and so sorely tried concerning his faith, Andrew Hewett was " faithful unto death." Well named Andrew, which means " manly " ! He was manly indeed for the Man Christ Jesus, and his courage should appeal to the young manhood of to-day.

XVII

CANTERBURY

Nicholas Shetterden—Stephen Kempe— Thomas Cranmer

WE might well linger more than a little while in the ecclesiastical capital of England. Apart from a nameless priest who was converted to the faith of the Gospel, and because of his faithfulness to Christ was burnt to death in 1498 by order of Henry VII., there are only two names known of Canterbury natives who were martyrs for the Protestant faith. There is little cause for wonder in this, considering that the city was the centre of Rome's sway in our land.

All the rest of the martyrs associated with Canterbury were from other parts of the county. From the various towns and many villages, the victims of Roman Catholic persecution were brought here to be tried and afterwards put to death. Men and women in different stations of life were taken. Clergy, ministers, and priests were among the number, and worthies were found in various trades. Nor were persons of wealth and culture wanting in fidelity to the Word of God, for three gentlemen were burnt at one time, namely, George Roper, John Webbe, and Gregory Parke, on November 30th, 1555.

CANTERBURY

Men and women, old and young, were alike true to their vows, and loyal to their Divine King.

Nicholas Shetterden is one of the names identified with Canterbury. His place of residence is unknown, but as he was, for long, a prisoner at Westgate, Canterbury, his name must be linked with this ancient cathedral city. Because of his firm stand for the Word of God, he was brought up again and again before his various judges, but, unswerving in his fidelity to the Protestant faith, he was steadfast to the very end. His examination before the Bishop of Winchester, the then Lord Chancellor, is well worth our consideration.

He left the report himself, which is as follows:

"I was called into a chamber before the Lord Chancellor, the Suffragan, and others. He stood by the table, and because I saw the Cardinal was not there, I bowed and drew near. Then said he: 'I have sent for you because I hear you are indicted for heresy; and being called before the Commissioners, you will not answer nor submit yourself.'

"I said: 'I did not refuse to answer; but I did plainly answer that I had been in prison a long time, and reason it was that I should be charged or discharged of that, and not to be examined of articles to hide my wrong imprisonment; neither did I know any indictment against me. If there were any, it could not be just, for I have not been abroad since the law was made.'

"WINCHESTER.—'If thou wilt declare thyself to the Church to be a Christian, thou shalt go, and then have a writ of wrong imprisonment, etc.'

"SHETTERDEN.—'I have no mind to sue now,

but require justice; but to make a promise I will not; and if I offend the law, punish me accordingly. For it might be that my conscience was not persuaded, nor would be in prison; seeing these things which I have learned were by God's law openly taught and received by the authority of the realm.'

"WINCHESTER.—'It was not a few that could be your guides in understanding, but the doctors of the whole Church; now, whom wouldst thou believe? either the few or the many?'

"SHETTERDEN.—'I did not believe for the few or for the many, but only for Him that bringeth the Word, and showed it to me to be so, according to the process thereof.'

"So after many words, by which he thought to ensnare me, he came to the Church's faith, and comely order of ceremonies and images. And then I joined to him again with the Commandments.

"WINCHESTER.—'That was done that no false things should be made, as the heathen would worship a cat because she killed mice.'

"SHETTERDEN.—'It is plain that the law forbids not only such, but even to make an image of God to any manner of likeness.'

"WINCHESTER.—'Where find you that?'

"SHETTERDEN.—'Forsooth, in the law where God gave them the Commandments; for He said, "Ye saw no shape, but heard a voice only"; and added a reason why, "lest they should after make images and mar themselves"; so that God would not show His shape, because they should have no image who was the true God, etc.'

MARTYRS' MEMORIAL, CANTERBURY

Photo by F. & H. Fisk-Moore, Canterbury] *[Facing page 64*

"WINCHESTER.—'You have made a goodly interpretation.'

"SHETTERDEN.—'No, it is the text.'

"A Bible was then brought. He bade me find it, and so I read it aloud; the place was Deut. iv. 12-19, 'And the Lord spake unto you out of the midst of the fire,' etc.

"WINCHESTER.—'Well, yet by your leave, so much as was seen you may, that is, of Christ, of the Holy Ghost, and of the Father, who appeared to Daniel like an old man.'

"SHETTERDEN.—'That is no proof that we may make images contrary to the Commandment; for though the Holy Ghost appeared like a dove, yet was He not like in shape, but in certain qualities; and therefore, when I saw the dove, which is God's creature, indeed I might remember the Spirit to be simple and loving.'

"At last he said he saw what it was, and that he had sent for me for charity's sake to talk with me; but now he would not meddle, and said my wrong imprisonment could not excuse me, but I must clear myself. I said that was easy for me to do, for I had not offended. He said I could escape so, there I was deceived.

"SHETTERDEN.—'Well, then, I am under the law.'

"The Archdeacon was then called in, and he said that I behaved myself before him with such arrogancy as never was heard; whereas he was minded with such mercy toward me; and many other lies he laid to me, that I was sent home till another time, and I would not be contented.

"SHETTERDEN.—'I declare that therein he falsely reported me, and brought in laws then in the realm, and the Queen's proclamation, that none of her subjects should be compelled till the law was to compel; and that I rehearsed the same in the Court for me. And I did use him then, said I, as I use your Grace now, and no otherwise.

"WINCHESTER.—'Well, you do conduct yourself very well now.'

"I said, 'I had so offered myself to be bailed, and to confer with them when and where they would.'

"WINCHESTER.—'You should not confer, but be obedient.'

"I said: 'Let me go, and I will not desire to confer neither; and when offended, let them punish me,' and so departed" (John Foxe).

He was afterwards brought up before his judges with his fellow-prisoners — John Bland, John Frankesh, and Humphrey Middleton. Nicholas Shetterden so baffled his judges that at last the Lord Chancellor, the Bishop of Winchester, said: "Who hath taught you so well?" Shetterden replied: "The Lord Himself!" He was condemned by the Bishop of Dover on the 25th day of June, 1555.

A few days before he suffered, he wrote an affectionate letter to his wife, and two to his mother, wishing her "increase of grace and godly wisdom." He also wrote to his brother, Walter Shetterden, expatiating on "the true faith and doctrine of Christ." In a last letter to his brother he breathed a manly spirit, worthy of the Great Cause for which he died. His brother had informed Nicholas that, if he would recant, he would bestow a large fortune on him. But wealth had no more influence than the fear of death, so the promised riches were refused, in the courageous spirit of a Christian hero, confident of the treasures laid up for him in heaven.

The farewell letter to his mother (signed and sealed with his own blood) was dated from Westgate, July 11th, 1555, the day before his martyrdom; and therein he pleaded with her to "beware of the great idolatry and the blasphemous Mass, and to follow the counsel of God's Word"—to trust Christ alone for salvation. It had also this P.S.: "Appointed to be slain for Christ's cause and the maintenance of His most sound and true religion" (Foxe, *Acts and Monuments*, vol. vii. p. 314).

He was led away to the Martyrs' Field with three others, on July 12th, 1555, and went to his eternal home by fire.

Stephen Kempe (burned January 15th, 1557) was another of the Protestant Martyrs. He is mentioned as "of Norgate," or Northgate, but of this brave witness for the Word of God little is known, except that he, too, was "faithful unto death"; and that, surely, is sufficient!

There is yet one more name inseparably linked with Canterbury and its Martyrs, namely, Archbishop Cranmer.

Thomas Cranmer was born at Alsacton, near Nottingham, on July 2nd, 1489. He came of a family whose ancestors arrived in England with William the Conqueror, and had resided at his birthplace for many generations. He received his first lessons in education from an old and inflexibly severe priest. On his father's death, the mother of Thomas placed him at Jesus College, Cambridge, where he applied himself with great diligence to his studies, especially to Hebrew, Greek, and theology. Under the influence of the University, his genius was discovered and developed. In due course he took his M.A. degree, and afterwards obtained a fellowship. In 1523 he was made Divinity lecturer, also examiner of the candidates for degrees.

So zealous was he for the promotion of the knowledge of Scripture, that he would not permit any to proceed with the Divinity course unless they were well grounded in the knowledge of the Bible. Cranmer set himself to know the truth as it stood between Roman Catholicism and Protestantism, and he felt that it could only be settled by the Bible and that alone.

"After three years spent in the study of the Scripture without Commentaries or human help, the darkness of Scholasticism, which until then had hung about him, cleared away, and the simple yet majestic plan of Salvation stood forth in glory before his eyes on the sacred page" (Dr. J. A. Wylie).

The question of the proposed divorce between Henry VIII. and Catherine of Aragon was being freely discussed, and he spoke his mind frankly, not imagining that his words would be heard beyond the Chamber where on one occasion he was conversing with two of his friends. "Why go to Rome?" he asked. "Why take so long a road, when by a shorter you may arrive at a more certain conclusion?"

"What is the shorter road?" inquired his friend.

"The Scriptures," replied Cranmer. "If God has made this marriage sinful, the Pope cannot make it lawful."

"But how shall we know what the Scriptures say on the point?"

"Ask the Universities," replied the Doctor; "they will return a sounder verdict than the Pope."

Two days later, Cranmer's words were reported to the King. He eagerly caught at them, thinking he saw a way out of his difficulties.

Cranmer's counsel was that "the appeal should be made from the Pope to God, and from the Church to the Scriptures."

With this idea, Henry at once agreed, not knowing that it was the formal and fundamental principle of Protestantism.

Cranmer was immediately summoned to the Court and made a King's Chaplain. He would, without doubt, have much preferred the calm of a country parish to the splendours and perils of the royal Court. Thus he began and carried on his work, which was to lead him to the Primacy of England and the higher glory of the stake at the end of his career. In January, 1533, he was appointed Archbishop of Canterbury.

After Henry VIII. had divorced Catherine of Aragon and married Anne Boleyn, the Pope pronounced excommunication on the King of England. But the monarch had already provided against that contingency by the passing through Parliament of the "Act for the Abolition of Papal Supremacy in this Realm." Henry VIII. then became Head of the Church of England.

The Archbishop used all his powers for the promotion and furtherance of such measures as might give permanence to the new order. The Bible was translated into English, and distributed among the people. A copy was placed in every parish church on a raised desk, so that all might freely read the Scriptures. More than once did Cranmer differ from the King, and had more frowns than smiles, but he pursued his course of uplifting the religious life of the nation.

Not all his deeds and decisions were commendable; in fact, some we strongly condemn; but considering that he was educated in the Church of Rome, we may well wonder at his grasp of the truth, and his advance toward the light in such dark days. On the death of Henry VIII., in 1547, Cranmer was one of the executors of His Majesty's will. He was a member of the Council, and served also in the Regency appointed to govern the kingdom during the minority of Edward VI.

Cranmer watched over the mental, moral, and spiritual welfare of the young King with keen and prayerful interest. He is said to have wept with joy when he marked the intellectual development and deep piety of the royal youth. The Archbishop's personal knowledge and love of the Bible would lead him to see that the coming ruler of the kingdom should know the Word and will of the King of kings. His influence evidently went far to shape the conduct and mould the character of the young Edward VI.

CANTERBURY

The exclusion of the daughter of Henry VIII. (Princess Mary), by the will of her brother, was a measure in which Cranmer participated; and he also joined the supporters of Lady Jane Grey in the plan for her to take the throne; but that, possibly, against his judgment. On Mary's receiving the Crown, she immediately dispatched a messenger to the Pope to announce her accession.

The Princess Mary owed a personal debt to Cranmer, who is reported to have preserved her from the anger of her father, which threatened her destruction because of her determined adherence to the faith and claims of the Church of Rome, but she could neither forgive nor forget. Cranmer was therefore destined to be the victim of her personal wrath and Papist hate. A number of Reformers, before espousing her cause as Queen, begged to know whether she were willing for the religious settlement effected under Edward VI. to continue. She bade them put their minds at ease, promising that no man should be molested on the ground of religion and that she would be content if she were allowed to practice in peace her own worship.

"These soft words smoothed her way, but soon she changed her speech and, throwing off all disguise, she left none in doubt that her settled purpose was the suppression of the Protestant faith" (Dr. J. A. Wylie, vol. iii. p. 420).

Without losing a day, she proceeded to undo all that her father and brother had done for the Protestant cause. She requested the Pope to send Cardinal Pole with full power to receive the kingdom back into the Roman pale. The last time Archbishop Cranmer officiated publicly was on the day when he read the Protestant burial service at the funeral of Edward vi. After this he was ordered to confine himself to his own house at Lambeth.

Cranmer was brought before the Commissioners in September 1555. Dr. Brooks, Bishop of Gloucester, and two delegates (Martin and Scory) came with authority from Cardinal Pole to judge him. He told the Commissioners he could never serve two masters, and that since he had sworn allegiance to the Crown he could not submit to the Pope. He also showed that "the Pope's power had been as unjustly used as it was ill grounded."

After much discourse on both sides, Dr. Brooks (the presiding Commissioner or judge) required Cranmer to appear before the Pope within eighty days, and answer the charges that should be brought against him. Cranmer said he would do so willingly, but he could not possibly go to Rome if he were kept in prison here.

In February 1556, Bonner and Thirleby were sent to degrade him for his non-appearance at Rome, although all the while he had been detained as a prisoner in England. He was clothed with all the episcopal robes, made of canvas, and then they were taken from him according to the ceremonial of degradation.

In all this the Archbishop was little concerned. He denied that the Pope had any authority over him, and appealed from his sentence to a free General Council. Many devices were made to influence him to recant, and both English and

Photo by F. & H. Fisk-Moore, Canterbury] CANTERBURY CATHEDRAL. [Facing page 72

Spanish divines had conferences with him. Cranmer was taken to Oxford and there imprisoned in the Bocardo. The Archbishop was afterwards removed to the house of the Dean of Christ Church. Crafty men gathered around him and treated him with much respect, professing their desire to prolong his life for future service and honour. They suggested that he might dictate his own words of submission. At last he recanted. "Alas! the man who stood erect amid the storms of Henry VIII.'s time, and had often ignored the wishes and threats of that wayward monarch, and followed the path of duty, fell by the arts of these subtle seducers" (Dr. J. A. Wylie, *History of Protestantism*). He signed the submission demanded of him.

The Queen and the Cardinal were overjoyed at the fall of the Archbishop. His recantation would do more, they thought, than all their stakes, to suppress the Reformation in England. None the less did they adhere to their set purpose of burning him, though they carefully concealed their intentions.

On the morning of March 21st, 1556, he was led out of prison, and, preceded by the Mayor and Aldermen, with Spanish friars on either side of him, chanting penitential Psalms, they conducted him to St. Mary's Church, there to make his recantation in public. "The Archbishop having already felt the fires that consume the soul, dreaded the less those that consume the body, and suspecting what his enemies meditated, made his resolve." He was placed on a platform before the pulpit, and there, in "the garments and ornaments" of an Archbishop, "only in mockery, for everything was of canvas and old clouts," sat the man who had, till lately, been the first subject in the realm. Dr. Cole preached the sermon, and at the end he exhorted the Archbishop to clear himself of all suspicion of heresy by making a public confession. To this Cranmer replied: " I will do it, and, that with good will."

He then rose up and addressed the vast concourse. He declared his abhorrence of the Romish doctrines, and expressed his steadfast adherence to the Protestant faith. "And now," said he, " I come to the great thing that so much troubleth my conscience more than anything that ever I did or said in my whole life."

He then solemnly revoked his recantation, adding, " Forasmuch as my hand offended, writing contrary to my heart, my hand shall first be punished therefor ; for may I come to the fire, it shall be first burned. And as for the Pope, I refuse him, as Christ's enemy and Antichrist, with all his false doctrines."

Hardly had he uttered the words when the Romanists, filled with fury, dragged him violently from the platform and hurried him off to the stake. It was already set up on the spot at Oxford where Ridley and Latimer had suffered in the previous year. Cranmer quickly put off his garments and stood in his shroud, with his feet bare, a spectacle to move the heart of friend and foe—at once a penitent and a martyr.

As soon as the fire approached him, he stretched out his right arm, and thrust his hand into the flame, saying, " That unworthy right hand." He kept it in the fire, excepting that he once wiped with it the drops of perspiration from his brow, till it was consumed, repeatedly exclaiming, "That unworthy right hand." The fierce flames now surrounded him, but he stood as unmoved as the stake to which he was chained (John Foxe). Raising his eyes toward heaven, he breathed out the prayer of the first Christian martyr, Stephen, "Lord Jesus, receive my spirit"; and thus the first Protestant Archbishop of Canterbury expired, and inscribed his name on the Martyrs' Roll. No marble tomb contains his ashes: no Cathedral tablet records his virtues. Nor are such needed, for, as Strype has well said: "His martyrdom is his monument" (*Memorials of Cranmer*, p. 371).

John Richard Green (*Short History of the English People*, p. 360), says: "It was with unerring instinct that . . . the Protestants fixed, in spite of his recantations, on the martyrdom of Cranmer as the death-blow to Roman Catholicism in England."

What more shall I say but that, ere we leave the historic city of Canterbury, we shall look again at the worthy Martyrs' Memorial and read the long list of heroes and heroines of the Cross, who rejoiced they were "counted worthy to suffer for the sake of the Name of the Lord Jesus"? They were all Martyrs for their Saviour, and now wear the Martyr's crown. Of them all it may be said: "The noble army of Martyrs praise Thee."

The Martyrs' Memorial consists of granite, and is a credit to Canterbury. On the front the inscription is as follows:

NOBLE MARTYRS OF KENT

In Memory of
FORTY-ONE KENTISH MARTYRS
WHO WERE
BURNT AT THE STAKE ON THIS SPOT
IN THE REIGN OF QUEEN MARY
A.D. 1555-1558.

FOR THEMSELVES THEY EARNED THE MARTYR'S CROWN
BY THEIR HEROIC FIDELITY THEY HELPED TO SECURE
FOR SUCCEEDING GENERATIONS THE PRICELESS
BLESSING OF

RELIGIOUS FREEDOM.

"PRECIOUS IN THE SIGHT OF THE LORD IS
THE DEATH OF HIS SAINTS."

NAMES ON RIGHT SIDE.	NAMES ON LEFT SIDE.
JOHN BLAND (Vicar of Adisham)	JOAN SOLE
JOHN FRANKESH (Vicar of Rolvenden)	JOAN CATMER
NICHOLAS SHETTERDEN	WILLIAM WATERER
HUMPHREY MIDDLETON	STEPHEN KEMPE
WILLIAM COKER	WILLIAM HAY
WILLIAM HOPPER	THOMAS HUDSON
HENRY LAWRENCE	WILLIAM LOWICK
RICHARD COLLIER	WILLIAM PROWTING
RICHARD WRIGHT	JOHN FISHCOCK
WILLIAM STEERE	NICHOLAS WHITE
GEORGE CATMER	NICHOLAS PARDUE
ROBERT STREATER	BARBARA FINAL
ANTHONY BURWARD	BRADBRIDGE'S WIDOW
GEORGE BROADBRIDGE	WILSON'S WIFE
JAMES TUTTEY	ALICE BENDEN
JOHN WEBBE	JOHN CORNEFORD
GEORGE ROPER	CHRISTOPHER BROWNE
GREGORY PARKE	JOHN HERST
JOHN LOMAS	ALICE SNOTH
AGNES SNOTH	KATHERINE KNIGHT
ANNE ALBRIGHT	

On the other side are the following words:

THIS SITE WAS GIVEN
THE SURROUNDING GROUND WAS PURCHASED
AND THIS MONUMENT WAS ERECTED
BY
PUBLIC SUBSCRIPTION
A.D. 1899.

LEST WE FORGET.

Before we say farewell to this sacred spot, with reverence we salute the names of the sainted dead. And let us pledge ourselves never to forget the price paid for our precious Protestant privileges, and resolve to help all to remember our incalculable debt to those who suffered in the past for truth and liberty.

We have not taken the chronological order of the martyrdoms, but for convenience have pursued the topographical path; wending our way from place to place we have sought to cover as far as possible the ground made dear to us in this fair county by the Martyr spirit. May we as Protestants value our liberties and privileges more dearly than ever, seeing that they have been purchased with so great a price—even the agony and blood of many of the saints of God—and determine that we too will be faithful in our day and generation; for, as Bishop Heber so inspiringly wrote:

> The Son of God goes forth to war,
>   A kingly crown to gain;
> His blood-red banner streams afar:
>   Who follows in His train?

Who best can drink His cup of woe,
  Triumphant over pain,
Who patient bears His cross below,
  He follows in His train.

The martyr first, whose eagle eye
  Could pierce beyond the grave,
Who saw his Master in the sky,
  And called on Him to save;
Like Him, with pardon on his tongue,
  In midst of mortal pain,
He prayed for them that did the wrong:
  Who follows in his train?

A noble army, men and boys,
  The matron and the maid,
Around the Saviour's throne rejoice,
  In robes of light arrayed;
They climbed the steep ascent of heaven,
  Through peril, toil, and pain:
O God, to us may grace be given
  To follow in their train!

"Be thou faithful unto death, and I will give thee a crown of life."—REVELATION ii. 10.

A PROPOSAL

IT is a matter for great regret that there is no monument in Rochester to perpetuate the memory of the four Protestant Martyrs connected with the ancient city on the Medway. It has long been the dream and keen desire of the writer of this book that a permanent record in bronze or stone should be provided for this purpose. He has therefore decided that out of the profits accruing from the sale of this volume, the cost of a suitable memorial tablet shall be defrayed; or better still, if possible, a worthy monument erected. The following is suggested as an inscription that might be used:

In Grateful Memory
of the Protestant Martyrs of Rochester

NICHOLAS HALL (of Dartford)
Burnt at Rochester, July 19th, 1555.

NICHOLAS RIDLEY, Bishop of Rochester
1547-1550
Burnt at Oxford, October 16th, 1555.

JOHN HARPOLE (of St. Nicholas Parish, Rochester)
JOAN BEACH (of Tonbridge)
Both burnt at Rochester, April 1st, 1556.

"Be thou faithful unto death."—Rev. ii. 10.

Every purchaser of this book may have the satisfaction of sharing in this desirable object, and all who read and recommend this story to others may know they have helped to attain this end. Thus, in the Cathedral city of Rochester, with its historic past, there would be a public and perpetual witness to commemorate the brave sufferings and heroic deaths of those who gave their lives for the sake of the Truth of God, and by so doing paid a large part of the great price in the purchase of the religious liberty which we all now enjoy.

G. A. M.

www.ingramcontent.com/pod-product-compliance
Lightning Source LLC
Chambersburg PA
CBHW020148170426
43199CB00010B/935